FIND THE FROGS

by Hugo Fable

From author Hugo Fable, comes a brand new, fun and entertaining book for kids!

Find the Frogs challenges curious young readers to - you guessed right - find the frogs!

There are several frogs cleverly hiding on each page!

From a water park to an ice cream shop, a pirate's cabin, and a tropical beach, this book has plenty of challenges and treasures in store.

Can you find the frogs?

Perfect for ages: 3 - 12 years and up.

Welcome to Hawaii!

With beautiful white sand beaches and fun palm trees to explore, do you blame these little frogs for skipping their hula dance class?

See if you can find the little frogs:

BLUE   PINK   YELLOW

Welcome to the tropical reef! This one has a mermaid's house and hidden treasure!

This yellow frog diver is looking for his little frog buddies. Can you spot them?

PINK   BLUE   GREEN

Frogs really love water parks!

Purple frog lifeguard is busy keeping the little frogs safe as they enjoy splashing around the pool!

Let's keep an eye on these little frogs:

YELLOW **GREEN** **BLUE**

Welcome to Blue Frog's Surf Shop!

Here you will find lots of surfboards to catch those big waves out on the ocean. You can also find some frogs hiding in this shop!

YELLOW   PINK   GREEN

After surfing the big waves, there's nothing better than ordering a pizza and playing your favorite video games!

These little frogs are full of energy!

GREEN   BLUE   YELLOW

Time to relax in the local frog pond!

These little frogs are not so good at hiding when it comes to just having fun!

PINK   **BLUE**   **YELLOW**

Welcome to Santa's Workshop!

The yellow frog is filling in for Santa's elves.

Can you help him find his little frog friends
so that they can start making toys for all
the good young boys and girls?

PINK   BLUE   GREEN

Welcome to the pirate's cabin!

This is Captain Blue Frog and he needs your help finding his shipmates! These little frogs are less about work and more about fun!

YELLOW   GREEN   PINK

These frogs live in a pumpkin house!

Farmer Purple Frog has a busy day ahead, and he will need help from these little frogs.

YELLOW   GREEN   BLUE

Welcome to the ice cream parlor!

Here you will find many flavors of ice cream,
lots of old-fashioned candy, root beer floats,
and three little frogs minding the store.

YELLOW   GREEN   PINK

Let's go back in time to see the dinosaurs!

Cowboy Blue Frog is riding on a T-Rex. Our little frog friends are not amused!

PINK   YELLOW   GREEN

Well that about wraps it up after a hard day at work for these little frogs!

All kidding aside, these little frogs do not like work! Can you find them?

BLUE   GREEN   PINK

GOOD JOB!

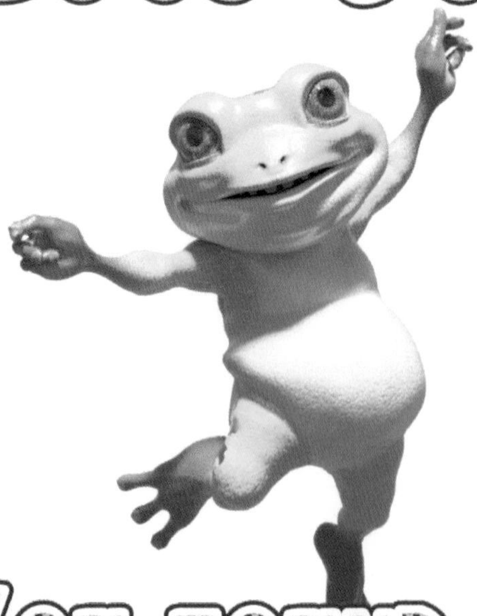

YOU FOUND ALL THE FROGS!

About the Author

Hugo Fable creates fun and entertaining children's books with 3D imagery for all ages.

You can find his collection of children's books on his Amazon page. Just search for author Hugo Fable at Amazon.com.

You can visit him online on Twitter (@hugofable).

Printed in Great Britain
by Amazon

36705564R00018